Landlord Pennies to Banker Dollars

Books by John Lee

Secrets of a Deal'ionaire – Creating Wealth One Small Deal at a Time (2014)

Secrets Those Credit Doctors Don't Want You to Know – 7 Simple Steps to a Higher Credit Score – Book and Workbook (2015)

4 Simple Steps to Prevent ID Theft and IRS Tax Refund Theft (2015)

How to Improve Your Credit Score – What Everyone Needs to Know (2010)

© HHLLC 2014, 2019. Secrets of a Deal'ionaire. Deal'ionaire OTC System Premier Signature Series. All Rights Reserved.

Landlord Pennies to Banker Dollars

7 Simple Steps to Fire the Landlord and Hire the Banker in You

SECRETS
OF A
DEAL'IONAIRE M.O.M.

By

John Lee

© HHLLC 2014, 2019. Secrets of a Deal'ionaire. Deal'ionaire OTC System Premier Signature Series. All Rights Reserved

Landlord Pennies to Banker Dollars

7 Simple Steps to Fire the Landlord and Hire the Banker in You

SECRETS
OF A
DEAL'IONAIRE M.O.M.

© HHLLC 2014, 2019. Secrets of a Deal'ionaire. Deal'ionaire OTC System Premier Signature Series. All Rights Reserved.

This information may not be reproduced, copied, stored in a retrieval system, recorded by video, audio, scanned, photographed, transmitted in whole or part, in any form by any means, electronic, mechanical, photocopying, recording or otherwise shared in any way whatsoever without written permission of the owner under penalty of law and remains the sole property of the owner.

This information is intended for illustration purposes only. Actual financial impact may vary as it may be affected by additional factors not considered in this information. The results generated by the strategies, methods, or techniques described in this information should not be used for any planning, forecasting or any other similar business purposes.

The information is provided "AS IS" without warranty of any kind, express or implied, and in no event shall the owner be liable for any damages whatsoever in relation with the use of this information. The participant agrees to indemnify and hold harmless and waive any liabilities or claims against the owner that result from this information.

Confidential — Non-Transferable Licensed Material © 2014, 2019 HHLLC. Secrets of a Deal'ionaire. Deal'ionaire OTC System Premier Signature Series. All Rights Reserved.

Dedication

This book is dedicated to all of the *Toilets, Trash* and *Tenants*. Without them I would have never learned all of the valuable skills that are the foundation of this book.

Acknowledgement

1st and foremost I want to acknowledge and thank my wonderful wife *Laura Lee*. As always, none of this would have been possible without her. Again, she turned chaos into something that makes sense. Laura has such an elegant way of making things come together and has the best *Smile* and *Pleasing Personality*. I don't know what I would do without her.

I would also like to say thank you to my many mentors, friends and encouragers.

A very special thanks to my good friend and mentor, 5x New York Times best-selling author, *Robert G. Allen*. Bob put the fire underneath me to write the first book in this series, "Secrets of a Deal'ionaire." In addition to coaching me how and what to write in that book, he also wrote the foreword for it. I am forever grateful for Bob.

Next I would like to acknowledge my best friend *AJ Rassamni*. AJ has led our mastermind group for over five years now. He is an excellent businessman and an expert marketer. AJ knows more about business than anyone I have ever met.

Meg Stefanac, my editor needs a special recognition also. Meg makes my words flow like no one else can. She has a way of simplifying my confusing grammar so even I appear as smart as a 5th grader.

And *Brenda Hite* needs an acknowledgement for the outstanding job she has done on the book cover again. She is a fantastic graphic designer and always does such a great job on my covers.

There are many more mentors, friends and encouragers that have helped me along this journey and deserve recognition. They are just too many in number and not enough room to list them here. I am deeply grateful and very thankful for each and every one of them. Thank you!

John Lee

Table of Contents:
Landlord Pennies to Banker Dollars

7 Simple Steps to Fire the Landlord and Hire the Banker in YOU

Secrets of a Deal'ionaire M.O.M.

Dedication	vii
Acknowledgement	viii
Introduction	xv
1. You Must Brainwash Yourself First	1
2. You Must Only Deal with Those Who Have Brainwashed Themselves	13
3. Why M.O.M. ?	29
4. STEP 1: You Are Not Renting a Dump… You Are Selling the Queen's Castle	47
5. STEP 2: You Must Know All of the Players	69
6. STEP 3: Your Network Equals Your Cash Flow	81
7. STEP 4: 1 + 1 = 27	97
8. STEP 5: Who Gets the Final Word?	109

9. STEP 6: K.I.S.R.S. 123

10. STEP 7: Landlords Work Hard…
Bankers Collect Easily 145

11. $ ♥ ☺ ☮ ♪ 🌴 2 U ! 163

Landlord Pennies to Banker Dollars

Introduction

"If you contemplate the Golden Rule, it turns out to be an injunction to live by grace rather than by what you think other people deserve."
~ Deepak Chopra

Are you a landlord? Do you know any landlords? Are you thinking about becoming a landlord? What is wrong with you?! Actually, there's nothing wrong with you. Being a landlord has made a lot of people very wealthy. It can be a very lucrative way to accumulate many assets and increase your cash flow.

I was once a landlord. There was a time when I thought being a landlord would enable me to retire with no worries. I figured that once I had a few good properties occupied by a few good tenants, I would be able to just sit back and collect my money. It would be easy-street, right? As it turns out, not exactly.

My intention here is to show you how I've eliminated a great deal of stress in my life by turning my rental properties into long-term wealth.

At the same time, I don't have problems with deadbeat tenants, trash, or toilets. I don't get calls in the middle of the night. I sleep well! You should, too.

In my first book of the Deal'ionaire OTC Signature Series, *Secrets of a Deal'ionaire*, I went into the details of how I have bought thousands of properties with little or no money out-of-pocket. In this book, I'm assuming you already have some properties, including rentals, or that you are considering buying some investment properties.

Once you get on a roll and get your system down, you can accumulate many properties easily. There are many books and courses out there that can show you how to buy properties, oftentimes very creatively. I encourage you to learn as much as you can.

The best thing you can invest in — the one thing that will actually help you reach your financial goals faster than anything else — is *you*. Invest in your education. Invest in yourself. Get a mentor. Learn from someone who has already done what you want to do.

There really is nothing new out there. There are just different ways of doing things. No matter what it is you want to do, someone has already done it, or at least tried to do it. Someone has already made the same mistakes that you are about to make if you go at it on your own. Why waste years of time making mistakes when you don't need to? Talk to others and learn from them. Learn it all; don't do it all.

An important lesson I've learned through my real estate experience that I'd like to pass on to you can be summarized in what I call the M.O.M. System.

M.O.M. Mortgage Option Management System

All right, so maybe you already know some of my Deal'ionaire strategies. You're probably wondering what is this M.O.M. System stuff? The M.O.M. system is an innovative way for you to fire yourself as a landlord and hire yourself as the banker.

I actually named the M.O.M. System after my own mother, Marie Lee (1939 – 2014) because it espouses her personal philosophy. My mom not only lived by the golden rule, she multiplied it.

Marie Lee treated everyone not just in the way she would like to be treated, but much-much better. She always acted with more compassion, empathy and respect than you would have believed possible — regardless of whether such kindness was merited or deserved. She did this even when she knew she would never be repaid. That was Mom. She made the world a better place just by being in it.

The lesson we can take from this: We reap what we sow. One good seed can grow a tree that produces delicious apples every year. The same is true with your real estate investments: when you plant good seeds, your investments can take root and produce real results.

It's Win/Win/Win! Because of M.O.M. we are *all* better off.

"If You Can't Trust Your Mom, Then Who Can You Trust?" ~ Anna Chlumsky

"[Luke:] I can't believe it.

[Yoda:] That is why you fail."

1. You Must Brainwash Yourself First

Chapter One

You Must Brainwash Yourself First

"Only Great Minds Can Afford a Simple Style."
~ Stendahl

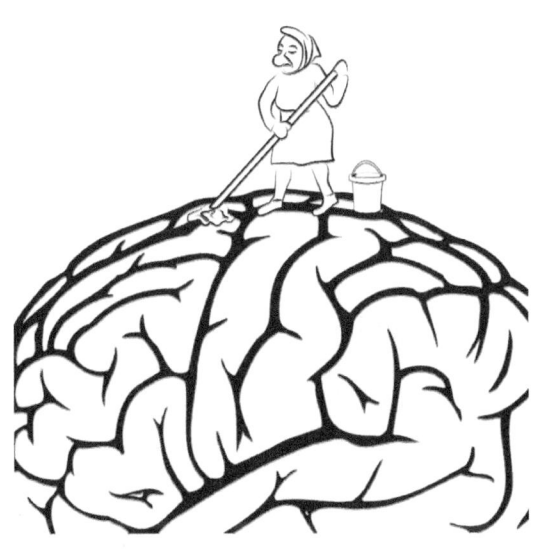

I know what you are thinking: "What do you mean I must brainwash myself first?" I am referring to your mindset. You must stop thinking like a landlord and start thinking like a banker.

Adjusting your mindset is your number one priority. It has to start with you. If you're not thinking with the right attitude, nothing will work out right in the end.

So, what does it mean to think like a banker? Well, bankers work nine to five. They don't take calls at home, and they don't worry about leaky toilets.

What do landlords do? They take calls at all times of day and night and they worry about things like leaky toilets.

Does this describe you? There was a time when it described me — but not anymore. Nowadays I am the banker. Think about it. Isn't wanting a better life the real reason we all got into real estate investing in the first place?

Life can be tough for all of us at times. Conversely, it can also be very good at times. Most of everything we get in our lives is due, in large part, to our attitudes, desires and what we focus on. We make our own choices and usually find what we are looking for — good or not-so-good.

One of the best things I have done for myself is not taking my cell phone into the bedroom at night. If something is really important, I'll hear about it soon enough. I find it better to block it all when I'm going to sleep.

It's the same thing with the news. I get it. You want to be up on current events, right? Unfortunately, too many people get obsessed with watching the news and overdo it. Trust me, when things are very important, you'll hear about them. Did anyone not hear about what was happening on 9-11-01?

The second-best thing I have started doing it taking the first hour of the day for myself. My good friend and mentor (and *New York Times* bestselling author), Robert Allen has taught me the importance of starting each day with "rich'uals." You have to change your habits in order to change your life.

Robert Allen and his son Aaron have created a great book called, *The Four Maps of Happy Successful People*, which I highly recommend. In this book, Allen goes into the details of how to set your life up for simple successes. I'm so old fashion that this was actually the first book I ever bought to read on Kindle™. I normally don't want to read things on my phone. I have to wear my glasses.

When you get your own copy of *The Four Maps of Happy Successful People*, you will learn to start drawing four maps a day, with pen and paper. That will put you on a path to being able to handle whatever comes your way. Is it still tough? You betcha! There will always be storms and whirlwinds and other obstacles that will make your journey difficult. However, when you draw your maps each morning, you'll be ready for whatever setbacks come your way.

Now, back to your mindset.

You are NOT a landlord. You are NOT a landlord. You are NOT a landlord.

Got it?

YOU ARE NOT A <u>LANDLORD</u>!!!

GOT IT !?!

You have to think in a different way than you have been taught to think. *You are not a landlord.*

At this point, you need to make sure you have an entity. Even if you are the lone island doing everything yourself, you need to set up an LLC, a trust, or some other kind of business structure that separates you from the business.

You are not a landlord. You are not an owner of rental properties. What you ARE is part of the management team. You work for the company. I do not own any of my properties. My companies own my properties. I am just part of the management team. Even if you are the only employee, you want to just work *for the company*. You always want that separation.

Where should you set up your company? Some folks will tell you to set up a Nevada corporation because it enables you to hide your identity and not pay as much in state taxes. Other will tell you to set up your corporation in Costa Rica; they say that allows you to avoid paying federal income taxes. I guess that's true.

Personally, I have chosen to set up my companies in the state where I live. I'm doing business here and I choose to pay my taxes here. Of course, I have a good accountant and I do take advantage of every possible deduction. Every *legal* deduction, that is. [1]

One of the major advantages that I have found of not being a landlord or an owner is that I do not have to answer questions on the spot. Unless it has to do with something that demands urgent attention, like, heating, air-conditioning, or water problems, I simply say, "We have a board meeting once a week. I'll get back with you about that after the meeting."

Now, sometimes my board meetings just consists of me sitting alone on my deck pondering. There were (and still are) times I when I was the only one in my company. At the same time, I remind myself that I do not personally own my company. I just work for the company and am part of the management team.

---

[1] Note: I am not an attorney, so please don't take legal advice from me. My recommendation is that you hire the best attorneys and accountants that are available to you. That's what I do.

For me, I prefer to play by the rules, and I do not want to be deceptive. It's very important to be transparent. My rule to this day is to not post anything on social media or the Internet that my Mom would not be proud of. Not just okay with, *proud* of!

Now, with all that said, let me get back to the important job of brainwashing you! You are now a banker! You are not a landlord! You will never, never, never, never, never, never, never be a landlord again! YOU. ARE. A. BANKER!

You do not have tenants. You have homeowners. You work with buyers, not renters. You are the lender. You create Win/Win/Win situations where everyone wins. If you cannot create value for everyone you deal with, you do not do the deal.

From this point on, you will collect your money and you will only take phone calls that are beneficial to you. GOT IT? As I said, you must brainwash yourself first.

After all, you want the best from your Mortgage Option Management system (your M.O.M.), right?

Landlord Pennies...

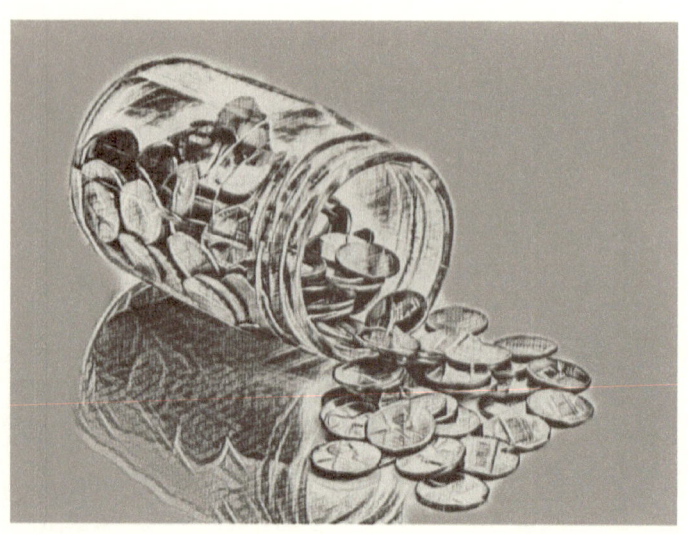

To...

Banker Dollars...

Your Choice...

2. You Must Only Deal with Those Who Have Brainwashed Themselves

Chapter Two

You Must ONLY Deal with Those Who Have Brainwashed Themselves

"People are not your most important asset. The right people are." ~ *Jim Collins*

In the last chapter we talked about changing our thinking. We are the bankers, not the landlords. In this chapter we will look at the mindset of the people we are making deals with. We are no longer looking for tenants.

Just like we brainwashed ourselves, we must *only* deal with those who have similarly brainwashed themselves. That is to say, it is important that you only deal with people who have the right mindset. We do not want tenants; we want buyers and proud homeowners.

So number two is look at the mindset of the people you are dealing with. Remember: No tenants; only owners.

The Problem with Tenants

The problem with tenants is, well, they're *tenants*. They have a renter's mentality. Many have the attitude that they are only leasing a temporary space and they treat your property that way. They operate under the attitude that they are going to move out in a year or so anyway, so why should they care about maintaining the home they are renting?

Why should they care if there's a leak under the sink? What do they care if their kids are skateboarding on the hardwood floors? What difference does it make to them if their dogs aren't trained to go outside and their cats are not using the litter boxes? Many simply don't care. And that's a big part of the problem.

In all fairness, there *are* some really good tenants. I've had the pleasure of leasing to many. Even though the percentage of bad renters is relatively small, you'll hear more stories about the bad ones than the good ones. This is because bad tenants are the reason for most of the pain involved with being a landlord. The M.O.M. system eliminates this pain.

Many tenants will remain tenants because that's the way they think of themselves. They do not want to change their mindset. Many are also training their children to think of themselves the same way. Some even believe that they're simply renting from the bad, rich landlord anyway, and that "He's got more money than us and he *owes* us."

Unfortunately, cities and municipalities also treat your properties like the *rentals*. When a neighbor complains about an abandoned vehicle or the grass being too high, they refer to the house as a rental.

Renters are very rarely held accountable for these complaints. The city goes after the landlord. Who's the landlord? Landlords are theoretically the rich investors who have plenty of money and time. Of course, that is usually not the case.

Most landlords are mom and pop operations that are investing just to get a little ahead in life. Few realize that many landlords put more time into this second job than they do into their full-time jobs and the other important parts of their lives.

So, what kind of mindset are we looking for in our clients? Not a renter's mentality. We are looking for *buyers*. We are looking for *homeowners*. We are looking for people who *want* to live in the neighborhoods where our properties are located. We are looking for people who will take pride in their homes and who will want to take care of it.

Say No to Rent-To-Own Lease Option Deals

To be clear, we are not looking for *Rent-to-Own* tenants. The problem with these people is they are still renting, and they are still tenants. They will treat your place like a rental. They know they can move out at any time. And they frequently do.

We are also not looking for *Lease Option* tenants. Again, these people are still renters. There are actually two problems with lease options: The lease and the option.

The *lease* has a specific time period, and your tenant can, and will, leave. The *option* makes this possible. Although your tenants may have the best intentions in the world, and although they may tell you how much they love the home and can't wait to buy it, many things can happen during this so-called option period that can put an end to these plans.

Also, it doesn't matter if your tenants are responsible for repairs. Repairs and maintenance responsibilities are included in many lease option contracts. You, as a landlord, might be thinking that this will take the burden off of you.

However, anything can happen. There may be an expensive repair needed, such as a new furnace or roof replacement. Tenants can, and will, walk away from a major repair. You might be thinking that because they have put down non-refundable option consideration money, this won't happen; but, most of the time, it isn't that much money. So, you got a few thousand dollars upfront. Often, by the time your tenants move out, it will cost way more than what you received in the deposit for you to fix your house back up.

The percentage of lease options that don't go through is as high as 97%. That's not very good odds. Even though you may be collecting 10 to 15 percent more than the market rents, in my opinion, it's just not worth the headaches.

I personally lost more than 25 thousand dollars on a lease option a few years ago. Someone came to me with a problem. He couldn't sell his house in the traditional way, that is to say, through a realtor. To make things worse, it was upside down, meaning he owed more to the bank than the home was worth.

Being the dealmaker that I am, I came up with a plan. I had taken a course on lease options many years earlier and thought I knew what I was doing. The course taught us that you should ask for ten or maybe twenty thousand dollars upfront. This is non-refundable option consideration money.

It all sounds really good until you start talking to the potential tenants. I couldn't find anyone who had ten or twenty thousand dollars for the option consideration. Many had only a couple thousand dollars. And that's what I ended up settling with.

During the three years that I optioned — and re-optioned — the house to potential buyers (who were actually tenants), I lost thousands of dollars. On my end, I was making the house payments that were higher than they should have been. On the other end, my tenants were *sometimes* making their payments, and they were tearing the house up.

Each time tenants moved out I would have to completely fix the house up. You landlords know what I'm talking about. I had to paint, redo the carpets, clean out all of the trash, get the yard and debris cleaned up. I did this three times in three years. No thanks.

And that's the main problem with mindset. These people considered themselves renters and tenants. They had a lease and an option.

I know this does not happen in every lease option case. I have many friends who use this investment technique and find it quite lucrative. Still, most of the time, their options are not exercised. The tenants usually move out.

Finding the Right People

All this is why we are looking for people who have a different mindset. What are we looking for? We are looking for a homeowner, a buyer, someone who wants to own a home. We are looking for someone who might have had some setbacks that make becoming a homeowner difficult.

Let's face it. We've all had ups and downs in our lives. I was a mortgage broker for many years. What

I found was that some of my favorite people to work with were those who wanted a second chance.

It seems that about every five to seven years we, as people, go through a major life change. None of us know what the future holds. We have divorces, deaths, disasters, and all kinds of other obstacles that we have no control over.

I've had many people come to me because they had some dings in their credit history and didn't know what to do. Bankers and mortgage companies simply look at their credit report and say no to a home loan. They may tell them to come back when their credit is better.

When people were serious about improving their credit profile, I would help them. Credit usually does not get tarnished overnight, and it does not get better overnight either. There were many times when I would work with people for a year or even longer.

For those who are interested, I have a good step-by-step book on improving credit scores. It's called *Secrets THOSE Credit Doctors Don't Want YOU to Know*. I still work with people and teach credit improvement today.

Some of the best people out there are the ones who really want a second chance. The key here is that they *really want* a second chance. There are many people who have gone through a divorce, a foreclosure, or a bankruptcy and appreciate the opportunity to turn their financial profiles around. These are the people you are looking for, because they tend to make the best buyers.

Of course, you still have to have your buyers screened and checked out. It still has to makes sense. You will ultimately decide whether or not to go through with the deal. We will get into more details on this in later chapters.

People who want to be homeowners but are facing difficulties are the buyers you are looking for. They tend to have the right mindset. You do not want anyone who says they want to rent to own. You do not want anyone who wants a lease option. You want a *homeowner*. You want a *homeowner*. You want a buyer. You want some one who wants to live in the neighborhood. You want someone who has pride in home ownership.

You want the mindset of the banker, not the landlord. You want your buyers to have the mindset of an owner, not a tenant or renter.

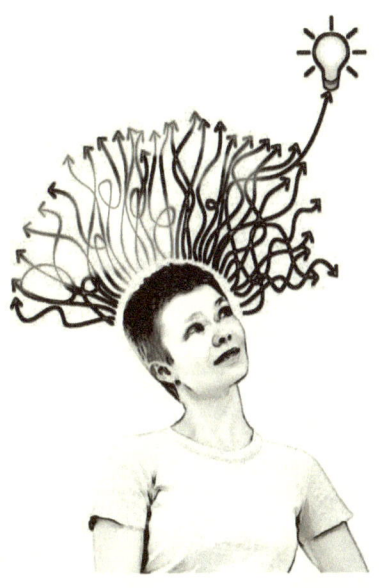

To reiterate: **You must ONLY deal with those who have brainwashed themselves!**

"Nothing can stop the man with the right mental attitude from achieving his goal; nothing on earth can help the man with the wrong mental attitude."
~Thomas Jefferson

Coming up:

Next we'll look at *Why M.O.M?* In this chapter, you will learn why to adopt the M.O.M. system, and why you can actually get more in house payment profits than from net rent proceeds. You'll also learn how to ensure that your buyers take care of the landlord's normal responsibilities such as maintenance, taxes, utilities, and other costs.

Landlord Pennies...

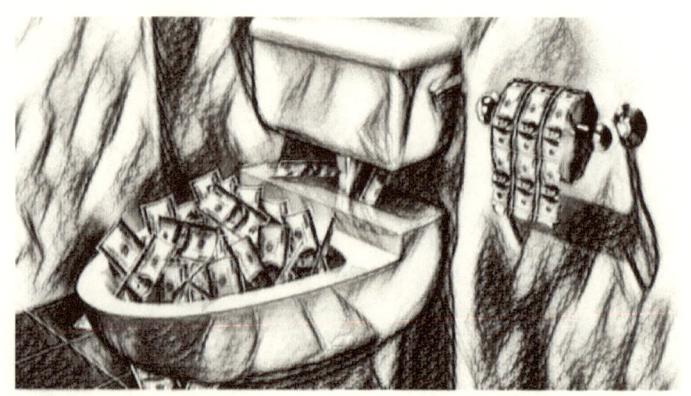

To...

Banker Dollars...

Your Choice...

3. Why M.O.M. ?

Chapter Three

Why M.O.M. ?

"You don't have to be a mathematician to have a feel for numbers."
~ John Forbes Nash, Jr.

Why would you want to be the banker instead of a landlord? Well let's take a look at the numbers using M.O.M., which is the fancy acronym for my Mortgage Option Management system. Let's compare landlord money with M.O.M. (or banker) money side-by-side. Numbers don't lie; people do.

We won't get into financing here. There are a number of ways to fund properties and many sources out there. There are several good private and commercial banks that have plenty of money. There are also hard moneylenders who charge more and are easier for you to get qualified with. You could also get partners to fund your deals.

Some lenders require down payments, and some have other terms with additional points and higher interest rates. Some go by the security of the property so you may not have to use your own cash or credit. For our purposes, we are just going to focus on the numbers. There is a difference between having a tenant and having a buyer. It's a huge difference.

We are also not going to be taking into consideration the cost to get an income property up and running. There are many factors that come into play with investment properties. You have repairs, holding cost, and a whole list of other things. We will just be comparing your landlord money to your M.O.M. (or banker) money.

First, the Basics

Typically, when we are looking at investment properties, we are looking at cash flow. Our first concern is **ROI** (Return on Investment). How much money are we going to get back from our investment in money, not counting our time and effort?

We must also consider the **CAP rate** (Capitalization rate). The CAP rate determines how long it will take to get your money back on your investment. If you have a CAP rate of 25% you will get your money back in 4 years.

Twenty-five percent is not always realistic. Many investors today agree that 10% is a good return on their money. It's not a bad return; but, personally, I like a little more.

There are a few other factors that are not always considered. We'll take a look a couple of them in a minute.

How are CAP rates determined? You take the **NOI** (annual Net Operating Income) divided by the purchase price. The NOI is the annual income minus your *expected* expenses. It can seem a little confusing, and it's a good starting place.

Don't worry. My experience has shown me that these numbers can be blown out of the water very easily. There are so many things that can happen to us—especially as landlords—both monetarily and emotionally. That's why we are moving toward firing ourselves as landlords and hiring ourselves as bankers. And we are changing from dealing with tenants to making deals with buyers and proud owners.

There are a lot of spreadsheets out there where you can simply plug in the numbers. Many dealers sell properties based entirely on their spreadsheets. The problem is that the figures can be manipulated in their favor to look good, at least on the spreadsheets.

Landlord vs. M.O.M.: a Hard Look at the Numbers

All right now that we have some basics, let's look at the numbers.

For simplicity's sake, let's take a look at the actual figures for a property valued at $100,000. This may be a high figure in some parts of the country and may be very low in other areas; but it's a round figure that is easy to work with when making comparisons.

The Numbers as a Landlord

Where I live, you can expect to get around $1,100 a month in rent for a rental property valued at $100,000.

As a landlord, you're going to have expenses such as taxes, insurance, management fees (unless you do the work yourself), vacancies, and repairs. You'll probably get a short-term renter of maybe one, two or three years. Then, you get to start over with a new tenant.

The cost for these miscellaneous expenses varies in different parts of the country. Repair costs and management fees depend on where your property is located. Insurance costs will vary according to such things as what area your property is in (ZIP code), the property's size condition and, your claims history, and (except in Maryland and Hawaii) even your personal credit score.

As a landlord, are ultimately responsible for most of these expenses. Tenants do not take care of your property the same way you do or an owner would. They may have a leak under the sink that goes on for several months before you are made aware of it. By then, not only do you need to replace the pipes, you also must replace the floor. Repairs are really one of the unknown factors when it comes to fixed expenses.

We don't have all that nonsense with buyers and owners.

In addition to repair costs, there are other unknown factors, such as vacancies. Those spreadsheets usually want you to input a fixed figure for vacancies just like they do for repairs. The problem that I've encountered is a property can sometimes remain vacant for several months.

When vacant, these homes may be broken into. When the copper pipes and air conditioning units are stolen, your profits go with them. It completely blows away your ROI for a few years.

The management fees are usually a constant. Of course, you can do everything yourself, including managing your rentals; but having done it myself, I don't recommend it. Research a few management companies thoroughly before making a selection. There's a huge difference between a good one and a bad one.

Personally, I don't care too much for spreadsheets. The problem I have with them is that they are easy to manipulate. With a little effort, you can put in any figures you want to get the outcome you want.

We get spreadsheets all the time from people wanting to sell their properties as investments. Some of the numbers make me laugh. I know the areas where many of these houses are located; and often, the numbers on these spreadsheets are tremendously fabricated to the extreme.

So, here's our $100,000 home that we put a lot of money, time and effort into. Let's look at our expenses, ROI, and CAP rate.

Landlord		Expense
Purchase Price		$ 100,000.00
Gross Rent		$ 1,100.00
Taxes	1%	$ 83.33
Insurance		$ 66.67
Management Fee 10%	10%	$ 110.00
Vacancies 10%	10%	$ 110.00
Repairs	10%	$ 110.00
ROI Per Month		$ 620.00
ROI Per Year		**$ 7,440.00**
Cap Rate		**7%**
Lease Term 1/2/3/ years		
Note Due to Owner		$

This is to say that after all is said and done (and provided everything goes as expected), we will get back 7%. That's kind of like me saying, if you give me $100 now, at the end of the year, if all goes well, I'll give you back $7.

The Numbers as a Banker

Okay, now let's look at some M.O.M. numbers.

As far as expense go, with the M.O.M. system:

* You don't have to cover the taxes because your buyer pays them.

* Insurance is optional, although I still keep it. (I sold a property to an investor a few years ago with owner financing. After about three years, I dropped the insurance. Little did I know the buyer had not insure the property. He evicted a tenant, and she burned the place down. She's now in jail—and I now keep my insurance.)

* You have no management fees.

* You have no repairs to cover.

What you *DO* have is a good ROI and CAP rate. You also have a long-term note and long-term cash flow. You will double and triple your money!

Homeowners have taken the place of my tenants and renters, and in doing so, have made my life so much easier. It's actually a great cash flow system minus all the stress that can come with being a landlord.

Let's look at the same $100,000 house comparing the M.O.M. system with the same ole landlord system that drove me crazy for years.

Notice the difference. You'll love the M.O.M. system.

M.O.M		
Purchase Price		$ 100,000.00
Gross Payment		$ 1,397.00
Taxes	0%	$ -
Insurance Optional		$ 66.67
Management Fee	0.0%	$ -
Vacancies	0%	$ -
Repairs	0%	$ -
ROI Per Month		$ 1,330.33
ROI Per Year		**$ 15,963.96**
Cap Rate		**16%**
Payment Term	20	
Note Due to Owner		**$ 335,280.00**

Not only is there a huge difference in your ROI and CAP rate, you don't have the stress of being a landlord. You don't have to fix things. You don't pay for things that landlords do. You don't answer calls in the middle of the night. You don't fix toilets!

Look at the amount we are getting back from our $100,000 investment. We are getting back more than $300,000! We are getting more than we would in rent. We have a long-term note for 20 years instead of a short-term renter!

Why Would Anyone Pay $300,000 for a $100,000 Home?

At this point, you might think, "Why would anyone pay $300,000 for a $100,000 house?" Several reasons. It's a great way for those starting out or re-starting out in life. When I was a mortgage broker these were some of my favorite clients.

They may not have 10-20% + closing cost and escrows to put down. Even the 3% down with FHA, other cost and all the hassles, may be too much. Maybe they have bad or no credit, recent divorce or their job history is too short. Many disasters happen to good people.

Maybe the big mean banks don't like them. Or, maybe they just want to be proud homeowners without all the *normal* hassles.

Let's compare:
Look at the difference. Are you kidding me?! Whoa!

Landlord		Expense	M.O.M		
Purchase Price		$ 100,000.00	Purchase Price		$ 100,000.00
Gross Rent		$ 1,100.00	Gross Payment		$ 1,397.00
Taxes	1%	$ 83.33	Taxes	0%	$ -
Insurance		$ 66.67	Insurance Optional		$ 66.67
Management Fee 10%	10%	$ 110.00	Management Fee	0.0%	$ -
Vacancies 10%	10%	$ 110.00	Vacancies	0%	$ -
Repairs	10%	$ 110.00	Repairs	0%	$ -
ROI Per Month		$ 620.00	ROI Per Month		$ 1,330.33
ROI Per Year		**$ 7,440.00**	**ROI Per Year**		**$ 15,963.96**
Cap Rate		**7%**	**Cap Rate**		**16%**
Lease Term 1/2/3/ years			Payment Term	20	
Note Due to Owner		$ -	Note Due to Owner		$ 335,280.00

So, do you want to be the **Landlord**...

Or...

The M.O.M. / Banker...

**Your choice...
You choose...**

By now, you are probably starting to understand why you want to be the M.O.M. (or the banker) instead of the landlord. We'll get into some details in the next chapter about making your home nice.

"Mind is a flexible mirror, adjust it, to see a better world." ~ Anonymous

We'll look at how you can make your home better than rent-ready, and why you can get more in *house payment profits* than *net rent proceeds*. I'll also show explain more about why our buyers take care of the landlord's normal responsibilities such as maintenance, taxes, utilities and other costs.

Landlord Pennies...

To...

Banker Dollars...

Your Choice...

4. STEP 1: You Are Not Renting a Dump...You Are Selling the Queen's Castle

Chapter Four

STEP 1: You Are Not Renting a Dump... You Are Selling the Queen's Castle

"In Every Woman There is a Queen. Speak to the Queen and the Queen Will Answer."
~ Norwegian Proverb

Earlier, we looked at modifying our own attitudes and mindsets. We also looked at the ideal mindset of the type of buyer we are looking for. In this chapter we are going to talk about the homes we are selling with the M.O.M. system.

We are not renting these homes, so they need to be *better* than simply rent-ready. Your home must look more appealing than all of the rentals in your area. Remember, we are looking for proud homeowners, not renters and tenants.

When we are dealing with tenants, we often do just enough when fixing up the property to make it rent-ready. We usually add a coat of fresh paint, clean the carpets, and have the place looking acceptably okay.

After all, this property is a rental. It may need some updates such as kitchen and bathrooms upgrades, but we may not want to put the money in it. As a general rule, renters are not as interested in how the house looks as buyers are.

This is not to say you have to do complete updates. Many home improvements cost more than you would get back selling the home the traditional way (i.e. by listing and selling it through a realtor and/or the MLS).

The MLS is the Multi Listing Service. The MLS is a place where all realtors can see any properties that you may have for sale. We will not be listing our properties in the normal, traditional way, so we will **not** be using the MLS.

I've discovered that many buyers and homeowners are willing and, actually, very happy to do their own updates. We've had many owners do some major updates at their own expense. We'll talk more about this later.

The important thing is that your home looks better than the rent-ready houses nearby. Remember, you are looking for buyers, not renters. Owners take pride in their homes and want to live in a nice place. These are the kinds of people we want living in our owner-financed homes.

Going for Maximum Curb Appeal

The first thing buyers usually see when they drive up to the residence is the front of the home. They look at the yard, the landscaping, and the front of the house. A lot of buying decisions are made in that brief moment. You do not want them to drive off without even getting out of the car to check out the home's interior.

There are many things you can do to give your property extra curb appeal. To begin with, don't have trash and debris, trashcans, dumpsters, hoses, tools or anything else that looks like you just did a quick rehab, lying around for them to see.

It's usually very obvious when you drive by a house and someone is in the process of, or has just finished, rehabbing a house. Many contractors do not clean up very well. Sometimes there are piles of trash, old furniture, televisions and all kind of junk that was left behind by the previous tenant. We, as rehabbers and landlords, like to put this stuff out by the curb.

Of course, as former landlords, we all know how these things go—and if you have ever had to evict someone, you *definitely* know what I'm talking about. Rarely does a tenant leave your home in the exact condition it was in when they were first handed the keys. This is especially true of evicted tenants. Evictions rarely end well.

In all fairness, there are some really good tenants out there who will leave your home without trash or damage; and many will even leave the property in broom-swept condition. At the same time, your house will still have normal wear and tear that is to be expected from someone simply living there. And if your tenants had children, there is generally a little more wear and tear.

Anyway, when your potential buyers pull up to the house, you want them to feel at home. You want them to imagine themselves coming home from work to a happy place. You want them to picture themselves living here and being proud to call this place home.

You want to make sure the yard is cut and trimmed, with no weeds or growth. You'll want to be certain there are no little trees growing out of the cracks in the driveway or sidewalk. You do not want the property to look unoccupied.

The next thing you want to be aware of is your landscaping. Are there a lot of trees, overgrown flowerbeds, or old bushes that have been there for decades? You want your buyer to see that a home that has been well-kept, not neglected. All too often, landlords do just enough to get their houses rented. Skimping on the yard is one way they save time and money.

Plant some fresh flowers by the front porch or along the driveway. Make sure the yard is tidy. You want to make your home look inviting. You want the buyer to picture their kids playing in the yard. You want them to feel that when they live in this home, they will be part of a beautiful community.

You can hire a professional lawn service or do the work yourself. I recommend using a professional lawn service. There are many around that do very good work at a reasonable cost. I've actually seen a service online that will cut your lawn for nineteen dollars. They'll even send before and after pictures so you can see their work no matter how far away you are.

Once you have the lawn cleaned up, you'll want to make sure that the front door looks good. It shouldn't have peeling paint or look beaten up. For some reason, the pros recommend having a red door. Red paint is pretty cheap compared to buying a new door.

I have bought my share of expensive front doors for the purpose of selling lower cost houses. There were many times when I have spent a $1,000 or more on a front door for a $25,000 house. And it paid off.

Many of these houses sold within a week. In most cases, though, you do not have to spend the extra money. A fresh coat of paint can do the trick.

Another important thing to consider is the appearance of the windows. You do not want prospective buyers to see broken panes or chipped and peeling paint on the frames. And, of course, the windows must be clean. A dirty window says a lot about your property and can influence how others view it.

The same goes with the garage door (if there is one). It needs to look nice and clean with no broken windows and no peeling or chipped paint. Again, taking the time to simply add a fresh coat of paint will go a long way toward improving your home's curb appeal.

Furthermore, the appearance of the mailbox is something that sellers often overlook. Whether it is out by the street or attached to the house, it needs to look good. Don't neglect your mailbox. I buy new mailboxes for almost every property that I sell. They don't cost that much.

Finally, you will want to have new, bright-and-shiny house numbers. Most cities and municipalities have minimum size requirements, and mandate that the numbers are prominently displayed. Shiny, new numbers will make the home show well, and will help your prospective buyers envision becoming proud homeowners.

Sprucing Up the Interior

Now let's go inside the property. When the future owners go through the front door, what will they see? It will usually be the living room.

Regardless of what room they are walking into, it needs to look good. The paint needs to be fresh. There cannot be any nail holes visible on the walls. And there definitely shouldn't be dirty fingerprints around the light switches. Like I said, it needs to look good.

One thing that many investors overlook is the smell. If you want it to sell, the home should have a pleasant aroma. There have been so many times when I've gone into a house and the first thing that I've noticed is a foul odor. Bad smells can drive potential buyers away.

Some houses smell musty or moldy because they've been empty for a long time. Some smell like paint. Some smell like cigarettes thanks to a previous resident or the workers and painters who have recently been in the house. Some homes actually smell like animals. It's hard to come up with a smell worse than cat urine.

Spend a little time to air the house out. Get some of those little pop-up or plug-in air fresheners. Put them in every room. They are only a couple of dollars each, and they can make a tremendous difference.

It almost goes without saying that *every* room needs to look good. The rooms need to look clean with freshly painted walls that have had all nail holes filled. Be sure to clean around all the light switches and outlets to remove dirt and fingerprints.

Speaking of outlets, you want to make sure the house does not have any cracked, broken or even just old-looking outlet covers. New outlet covers and light switches can be bought so inexpensively these days. In most of the homes I prepare for selling, I usually replace them all. As I said, the house needs to look good.

It's always good to know your target audience. In general, men and women are looking for different things in a prospective home. If you are expecting a couple to move in, you will want to make sure that your house can meet both partner's expectations. (Of course, the following are broad-view generalizations, and will not apply to ALL women or ALL men.)

Appealing to a Woman's Sensibilities

For most women, the most important room is the kitchen. Followed by the bathroom and master bedroom.

The Kitchen

The kitchen should be clean. There should be no cracked tiles or damaged backsplashes. The paint should look fresh, and there should be no offensive odors coming out of the drain or otherwise in the air. The kitchen floor, counter tops, and sink need to be clean and sparkling. Make sure your painters haven't left dirt or paint in the sink from their brushes being washed out.

The cabinets should be without broken hinges, scratches, nicks or dings. You don't necessarily have to replace them. In many cases, cabinets can be resurfaced or painted. Many contractors call this "repurposing" nowadays. Of course, if the kitchen hasn't been updated in a while or still has the old metal cabinets that were so popular in the '50s and '60s, you may want to spend the money and replace them.

If you are including appliances such as a stove, dishwasher, and refrigerator, they must also be sparkling clean. They should not have remnants of old food, stains, or cooking scars on them.

Sometimes it's easier to just replace those metal rings on the stove than it is to clean them. You know, the ones that catch the grease underneath the burners. They're not very expensive and they can give a new look to a used stove. Make sure the oven does not include old, burnt, over-flowed food that was left by the previous gourmet cook. It needs to look clean and should be free of obnoxious odors.

The dishwasher must also be clean. I can't tell you how many times I've opened up a dishwasher only to see dirt and things in the bottom such as labels off of jars. A dirty dishwasher can also have a foul smell. It doesn't take too much work or time to have a clean dishwasher.

The same goes for the refrigerator. I've seen many instances where the food left behind by the previous occupant was simply removed, but the fridge itself wasn't really cleaned very well. An uncleaned fridge can really stink. Some have even had food and beverages left behind by the contractors and painters. You want your refrigerator to be empty, clean, and have no bad odors.

The Bathroom

Typically the next room a woman will be interested in is the bathroom. The bathroom needs to look inviting. Give it a fresh coat of paint, and make sure it does not have any chipped, loose, or missing tiles. It also needs to be sparkling clean. There cannot be any paint residue in the sink, no fingerprints on the faucets, no old bars of soap stuck to the soap tray, no mildew in the shower, and no soap scum on the bathtub walls. And, I'll say it again; it cannot have any offensive odors.

Also, replacing faucets and showerheads is an inexpensive way to spruce the room up a bit. Sure, you can spend hundreds of dollars on one of those cool new faucets that are available these days, but you can also spend $30 or $40 on a basic one that looks nice enough.

Finally, make sure there is a fresh roll of toilet paper on the holder. I actually keep a four pack of toilet paper in the back of my truck at all times. It's saved me more than once if you know what I mean.

The Master Bedroom

The next most-important room for most women is the master bedroom. As before there cannot be any visible nail holes or blemishes on the walls. You must have fresh paint and clean floors.

The closet should be inviting. There should not be any old hangers or anything else left behind by a previous resident, such as shoes or clothing or garbage. It is not uncommon for sellers to neglect the closets. Many don't even paint them. It's very important that the closet looks and smells good. When a woman likes the closet, she will envision her clothes hanging in there. She will see her shoes lined up just the way she likes them. Turning to the room, she will envision her bed, dresser, and personal belongings arranged just so. She will also see her pictures and decorations on the walls.

A woman will typically spend a good amount of her time in her home. This is her castle, and she is the Queen. Regardless of what anyone says, a woman will have the most influence on whether or not her family buys the house.

Making the House Appealing to Men

What about men? Men look at houses in a totally different way than women do. In fact, they look at *many* things differently—but we're not going to get into that in this book. If you want to dig deeper into this subject, you may want to pick up a copy of John Gray's, *Men are from Mars, Women are from Venus*.

We've all heard of the "man-cave." Basically, it's a man's retreat, his hideout, a safe spot in the home where he can escape from the rest of the world. Where is this sacred spot? It's not a literal cave, of course (although, I've seen some real caves that looked much better than some man-caves I've encountered!).

A man-cave can be found in the basement, garage, workshop, extra bedroom, or even the shed out in the back yard. When men are looking at a home, they are usually most interested in the garage and the basement.

The Garage

In the garage, your prospective buyers will picture their parked vehicles. They will visualize their tools on the walls. They may see their kids' bikes, sleds and toys hanging from the ceiling.

You want to make sure that the garage is clean, with no oil or grease spots from previous occupants' leaking cars. As far as odors go, you do not want the garage to smell like a dirty garage. Have you ever had your car worked on at a dirty shop or a garage that smelled like it hadn't been cleaned in decades? It's a turn off.

Animal odors are another thing you need to be wary of. Some people keep their pets in the garage. I've been in homes that were pretty clean and did not have too many offensive odors, only to open the garage door and find myself pounded with pet stench—sometimes even spotting things like feces still on the floor.

You want your garage to be inviting with no unnatural odors. It doesn't necessarily have to have a fresh coat of paint, although that can often make a world of difference. A little fresh paint can go a long way.

The Basement

Let's move onto the basement. The basement is usually the second most important place in the home for men. Whether or not it is a finished basement is usually not as important as its condition.

First and foremost, the basement needs to be clean and with no old furniture, appliances, junk, or other debris left behind by previous occupants.

Basements can be a little more challenging when it comes to odors. Many basements, especially when they are in older homes, can smell moldy or musty. Many haven't been aired out in years, if ever at all.

Make sure that there are no water leaks, not only in the whole house, but in the basement in particular. Even a small water leak can cause mold to grow, and that can have a very obnoxious odor. Unless a leak has been ongoing for quite some time, most molds can be cleaned up fairly easily. There's only active mold if there's a water source. Fix the leak, clean up the mold, and that should take care of it.

A clean floor and fresh paint will go a very long way toward making the basement into an appealing man-cave. And keep it simple and clutter-free. The men, just like the women, will need to envision their own personal things there.

Your buyer is going to fill his man-cave with his own personal treasures. He will be putting up his own posters and displaying his own sports memorabilia and trophies. He may even be adding a pool table or a poker table. If there's a lot of junk lying around in the basement or it's dirty and smells bad, your potential man-caver will not be able to picture his belongings in the space, and that could cost you a sale.

Workshops/Sheds

A couple of other areas that men will be interested in are a workshop area and a shed if the house has them. Workshops are typically located in the basement or garage. Some can be found in out buildings such as sheds.

Regardless of where the workshop is, if your house has one, it needs to be clean, have fresh paint, and no offensive odors. Workshops and man-caves go hand-in-hand. Remember, we are selling these homes to buyers, not dealing with tenants.

To Stage, or Not to Stage? That is the Question

What about hiring a professional staging company? Many professional staging companies are very good at what they do. A staging company can strategically arrange furnishings in your home, setting it up to look spectacular for a quick sale at a top price.

You have to weigh the cost of the staging company against how much money you will be getting upfront. It can cost anywhere from several hundred to several thousand dollars to use a staging company.

So, should you do it? As with most aspects of real estate investments, it depends. It is something to consider in certain situations, but often isn't necessary.

Behold! The Queen's Castle

Following a few basic tips — such as ensuring cleanliness, fresh paint, and no obnoxious odors — should make your home more appealing than the others that your potential buyers have looked at. These tips will make your home better than rent ready.

Remember: You Are Not Renting a Dump...You Are Selling the Queen's Castle.

"Here's My Whole Marketing Idea: Treat People the Way You Want to be Treated."
~ Garth Brooks

In the next chapter, I will talk about discovering your environment, your neighborhood, your area, and answering the question, who is it that can make your life easier or harder?

Landlord Pennies...

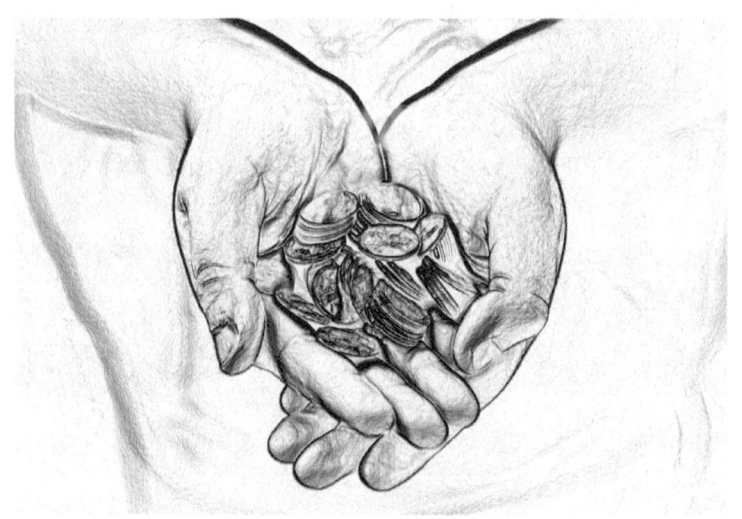

To...

Banker Dollars…

Your Choice…

5. STEP 2: You Must Know All of the Players

Chapter Five

STEP 2: You Must Know All of the Players

"It's Unbelievable How Much You Don't Know About the Game You've Been Playing All Your Life."
~ Mickey Mantle

Be aware of your community. You must know your environment—and you must know all of the players in it. These players can either make your life easier or harder.

So who will you be dealing with? You may think that you will only be dealing with your new buyers. Not quite so. There are many others who come into play any time you are investing in real estate.

The location (state, county, city, and municipality) in which your property is located will determine the people with whom you will be dealing. Or, I should say, the people who will be dealing with you.

What we're really talking about here are government employees to enforce the local regulations and requirements. There will most likely be city inspections; occupancy permits, zoning ordinances, and all sorts of other regulations that are enforced wherever your properties are located.

Get to know the people who are in charge. They are your counterparts. They can be your friends. Many property owners become frustrated and annoyed by the thing's inspectors fail their properties for. It if happens to you, don't get upset by it.

Sometimes, inspectors appear to have negative attitudes and it may seem that they are taking their issues out on you. It may or may not be personal. You don't know what kind of a day your inspector has been having. If you're just another crabby inspectee, you may find yourself the recipient of any violations they can find. Oftentimes, it seems that these inspectors just want to justify their jobs. It's usually best to be known as someone who complies with what they want. Sure, the cited violations often seem very petty, and sometimes the repairs they want don't seem to make any sense. Just go with it. One time, I actually had an inspector tell me he was having a bad day and it would be best to reschedule. I did; and he was very nice on his next visit. He still found a couple of things we had to fix though.

I've found that it's always best to become friends with the inspectors whenever possible. I find it necessary to insert a word of caution here: Do not bribe them and do not offer anything for them to look the other way on a violation. Simply being nice can go a long way and will let you sleep at night.

A Word about Houses in Historic Districts

Some properties are in designated historic districts. These properties can sometimes be a little challenging. Many communities have what are known as *preservation rules* wherein you can only use certain materials that conform to the historic integrity of the home.

You'll want to check with the housing division in the area in which your home is located to see what you can and cannot do when making renovations. Some places do not allow you make updates using new materials, like vinyl or asphalt shingles. You can only make replacement using the same kinds of materials that were original to the house, like wood, cedar shakes, or tile roofs. This holds true even though newer materials are often more efficient and would make big improvements to the home.

A few years ago, a friend of mine went to a small town in the South where she invested in several homes that were in dire need of repair. She started fixing up the houses, and in no time a code enforcement officer came and shut down her crews in the middle of their work.

My friend had been installing new siding and windows on one house, was in the process of having the siding torn off another and was treating her other houses with a fresh coat of exterior pain. She was told she could not use these new materials because doing so was in violation of the town's *Historic Preservation Ordinances*.

When she met with city's preservation officers, they turned out to be two little old ladies. These two women had all of the say regarding what improvements could and could not be done to homes in the historic district. During their meeting, my friend found out that these women even controlled what colors you were allowed to use when painting your house. And she was using the wrong colors on two of them!

After a couple of meetings, they were able to reach a few agreements. However, the changes that she still needed to make to stay in compliance ended up forcing my friend to go so much over her budget that she was barely able to break even when she finally sold the properties. What should have been a few quick-turn profits turned into months of aggravation with very little pay-out.

My dad had a similar experience when I was a child. He bought an old building and opened up a music store in what was then a small town in the suburbs of St. Louis.

After several years in business, he decided to do some updates and improvements to the building. It was, after all, more than a hundred years old, and it needed a few things done. He got some bids and hired a company to do the improvements.

After about a week, when the company was about halfway done with the project, a code enforcement officer came and shut them down. The building improvements, apparently, weren't *historically preserved* enough.

Although the updates resulted in a great improvement, they were not up to the historic standards that the local ordinances required. So the workers had to tear down what was already done and replace everything with *approved* materials. If my father had known to check ahead of time, it would have saved him a lot of money and aggravation.

Not only did his failure to know the local ordinances cost him a lot of extra money, it also cost him a lot of business. He could not have his doors open with the building in the torn-up shape that it was in while renovations were being done. He lost a lot of revenue because, for a couple of weeks, he could not teach music lessons or sell pianos, trumpets, clarinets, guitars or anything else, including guitar picks.

So, as I said in the first sentence of this chapter: be aware of your community.

A Quick Recap

So, to summarize, you need to learn about the communities where your properties are located, and you should take the time to find out who you will be dealing with while working on the houses. A little bit of homework and due diligence upfront can save you thousands of dollars and prevent you from having to deal with avoidable frustration and heartache.

Chances are, you are reading this book right now because you are tired of being a landlord. So, since you have probably already owned the property for a while, you likely already know about your community and its ordinances. Just keep all this in mind if you buy another investment home in a new area.

You Must Know All of the Players. Period.

"Always go into Meetings or Negotiations with a Positive Attitude. Tell Yourself You're Going to Make the Best Deal for All Parties." ~Natalie Massenet

Coming up we'll be going over Step 3, where I will talk about why it might be best to hire professionals to do some of the things you can (and do) currently handle yourself. We'll also look at why your network really does influence your cash flow.

Landlord Pennies...

To...

Banker Dollars...

Your Choice...

6. STEP 3: Your Network Equals Your Cash Flow

Chapter Six

STEP 3: Your Network Equals Your Cash Flow

"If you think it's expensive to hire a professional to do the job, wait until you hire an amateur."

~ Red Adair

How can your network have anything to do with your cash flow? Well, you can DIY (do it yourself) or you can hire professionals who can do it better. The latter will give you more time for working *on* your business instead of *in* your business.

Hopefully, by now you have begun to get your head on right by making the intentional mindset transfer from landlord to banker. You are ready to start replacing your tenants with buyers and proud homeowners. So, how do we get these proud homeowners?

When I first started buying investment and rental properties, I wanted to save money by doing all the work on my own. After all, I had owned a few businesses in the past and I knew how to do most things myself.

Initially, I would find the properties, buy them, and fix them up for rent all by myself. I ran the ads, met the prospective renters at the houses (even holding open houses on Sundays, my 1/2 day off), screened the applications, met the inspectors, filled out leases, took the phone calls, fixed the toilets, and collected the profits if and when there were any.

Of course, there were profits; otherwise I wouldn't still be in this great business called Real Estate Investing. The problem was, I was doing everything myself, and that can be exhausting.

One of the most important things I have learned about real estate is that it pays to learn as much as you can. I attend as many seminars and conferences as I can in order to learn from the experiences of others. I also make it a point to attend Real Estate Investment meetings so that I can keep up on the latest trends, updates, and knowledge.

One of the things I've learned by listening to those who have been in the business longer than I have is that you'll go further and get there much quicker if you gather a team of people who can do things better and more efficiently than you can. As my friend AJ Rassamni says, "Hire people that play at what you work hard at." Don't do it all yourself because doing so can be very limiting.

Why Hire a Property Professional

When you are ready to get a buyer for one of your homes, you can greatly benefit from hiring a professional to find that person for you. Sure, you could probably do it yourself; but in most cases, an experienced professional can do it better. You want to hire someone who is objective, and not emotionally attached to your property, as you may be.

So where do you find this professional who will get you the proud home-owning buyer you seek? I usually start by asking around at the real estate investment clubs and associations in the area where the house is located. The members who attend these meetings generally know who's who in this business. They will know who the good professionals are—and they can warn you about the bad ones that you should stay away from.

I like working with property managers. These professionals can run ads, show your property, and do preliminary screening of potential buyers through background and credit checks.

Whoever you hire, make sure to let this person knows right off the bat that you are looking for buyers and homeowners. You are Not interested in doing a *lease option* and you are definitely Not looking for a *rent-to-own* client. I usually tell my property managers that I don't even want to talk to someone who uses these terms. It is extremely important that your property manager or agent is completely aware of what you are trying to do.

You may be wondering how long it might take to find and close a deal with a qualified buyer. In my experience, it typically takes about as long as it does to get a qualified renter. It typically takes a month or two, depending on the desirability of the area that your property is located in. Of course, as with all things real-estate, sometimes it takes much more time than expected, and sometimes it takes much less.

One of the really nice things about hiring a professional is the fact that they really know what they are doing since they do this every day for a living. Back in the days when I tried to do everything myself, I would prepare the home, run the ads, and meet the people on my own.

Frequently, I was busy doing something else when prospective tenants called. (I was still a landlord in those days.) I would always drop whatever I was doing and go meet them. I don't have to do that anymore.

Another great thing about working with a professional is that these people are experts at screening. They know the right questions to ask on the phone before even deciding to meet with the prospect. They create applications that include all the right questions. They also have access to agencies that perform the necessary background and credit checks.

So, what kinds of fees do they charge for this service? Costs can range significantly depending on where in the country they work. There are also different ways they may charge you. Some charge by the month, some charge bi-weekly, and some charge a flat fee. By asking the investors who are members of the local real estate clubs and associations, you can find out what the going rates in that area are.

I always make sure that I set my pricing, so my professional screeners get their fees with plenty to spare. They will typically take their fee upfront.

We require the buyers to remit two monthly investments (payments) upfront as well as what we refer to as a *"low down payment."* I say **low** down payment because I want the buyers to tell us what they have to work with. If you give someone an exact dollar figure, that is what you will get.

I've found that, more often than not, buyers will offer more money for the down payment than I would have requested. By getting two months' deposit and the down payment, you will have enough cash-on-hand to pay your professional screener and get started.

A Word of Warning

Make sure you get a *good* professional. There are a few bad apples out there and working with them can lead to a nightmare scenario. A few years ago, I hired one of those bad apples. We'll call her Maria A. On the surface, her company looked legitimate.

I came across Maria A. through a Meetup group. (If you're unfamiliar with Meetup, it is an internet site that enables people with similar interests to organize online groups and local meetings.) The group I was in was a real estate investment club in my town. Maria A. had posted many times about her property management business in the group's forum. This is a very common way for people in the industry to converse these days.

I had a home that was ready to go, and I decided to contact Maria A. about her services. I told her that I was looking to sell the house with owner financing and needed someone to do the screening and show the property. She told me that that was exactly the type of service she offered. She also offered ongoing property management. That part I did not need.

Within a few weeks Maria A. had sent me a few prospective applications. The first few had a couple of issues that were a bit more worrisome than I wanted to deal with. After about a month, Maria A. sent me the application of couple that looked pretty good. We decided to go with them.

I met the couple at the house along with Maria A.'s assistant, a man I'll call Adam S. Up until that point, everything was going great. It seemed like Maria A. had a smooth-running business. She collected the buyers' deposit and down payment, and gave them the keys.

And that's the last I heard from Maria A. and Adam S.

They disappeared with all of the money. They were supposed to keep their portion (to cover their fees) and send the rest to me along with the paperwork. They kept it all—and they did not answer my calls.

I finally received the paperwork about two months later. It was incomplete, leaving out a lot of very important information I needed such as the buyers' dates of birth and social security numbers. It was also missing some important forms such as the authorization to release information.

To make matters worse, Maria A. and Adam S. had run off with the buyers' money, so I could not give them credit for it.

I went to the *Better Business Bureau* first. They informed me that they'd received several complaints about this company as well as some other companies that Maria A. had operated over the last few years. None of these businesses were real businesses.

Next I went to the *State Real Estate Commission*. There, I came to find out that Maria A. didn't even have a real estate license. I also learned that because she wasn't licensed, there was nothing they could do. They did send her a letter, which I'm sure ended up being filed in the round filing cabinet (her trash can).

After that I went to the local police to fill out a report. They were not very interested since it was only a couple thousand dollars. Also, it turns out that Maria A. had collected some of the money at the house and had then met the buyers at their bank to get the rest of the money. This bank was in a different municipality, so out of their jurisdiction. So now, this involved bringing in another police department. No one seemed to be interested. It was not a big enough crime.

So, needless to say we lost our money. Maria A. had been operating under a number of different business names and stealing from people for years. Last I checked she is still operating a business today.

What baffles me is how she manages to get credit reports and do background checks on people. When I was a mortgage broker, I had to go through quite a few checks on myself before I could get credit reports.

It had never occurred to me to ask Maria A. if she had a real estate license. She had been doing this for years, after all. Have you ever asked anyone for his or her professional license? I've never asked my attorney, my insurance agent, my doctor or anyone I can think of to see a copy of their license.

Be Sure to Research your Property Managers Well

My best advice is to verify that the professional you hire is for real. Get references from others who have used his or her services. Take some time to Google them and read online reviews. Check with the Better Business Bureau.

Most professional screeners and property managers are good people who are good at their jobs. Just be wary of the few bad apples.

In Summary

Your Network Equals Your Cash Flow. Hire professionals. In the long run, they will save you money by freeing up your time to pursue additional opportunities and investments.

"Never Hire Someone Who Knows less than You do About What He's Hired to do." ~Malcolm Forbes

In the next chapter, I will discuss marketing. Even though I hire a professional who provides pretty good marketing services for me, I enjoy doing some of it myself.

Landlord Pennies...

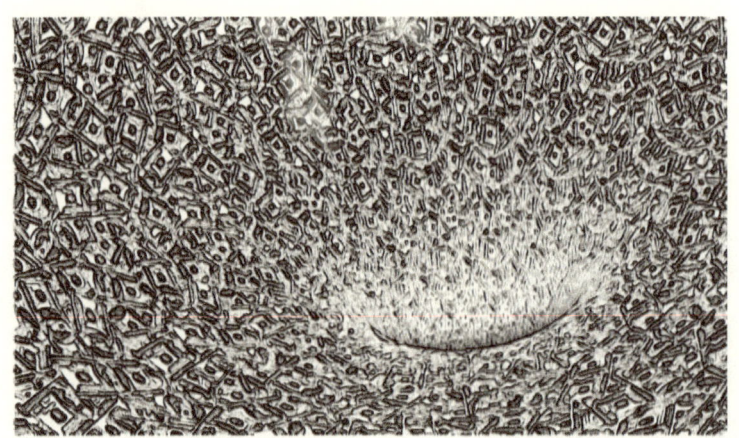

To...

Bankers Dollars...

Your Choice...

7. STEP 4: 1 + 1 = 27

Chapter Seven
STEP 4: 1 + 1 = 27

"Marketing is a Core Part of Anything You Do."
~ Keith Belling

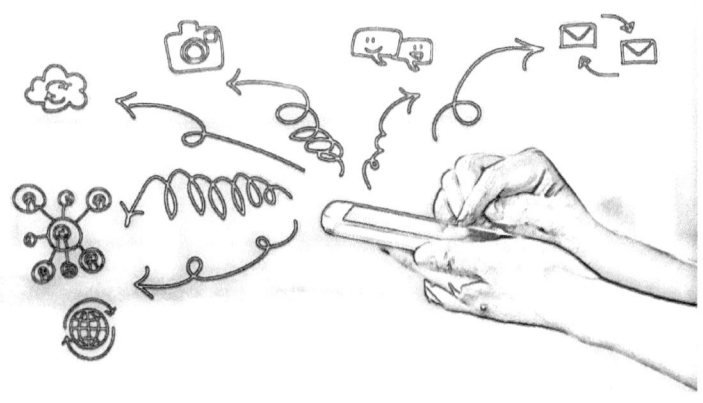

I know what you're thinking: "How could one plus one possibly equal twenty-seven?" Well, it's easy. It's what's going to happen when you participate in and control your marketing. You will increase your number of prospective buyers by running multiple ads that are *in addition to* your professional screener's ads.

In my experience, your professional screener will get around thirteen calls a day about your property. *You*, on the other hand, will generate about fourteen inquiries per day. Why will you get more? It's because your ads will look like FSBO (For Sale by Owner) ads rather than commercial ads. Often, the buyers you are looking for prefer to deal with individuals over companies.

So, that's **one professional** publishing ads, *plus* **one seller** (you) running ads, and it *equals* a potential **27** inquiries a day. 1 + 1 = 27. Simple math (though your first-grade teacher might disagree!).

Getting the Word Out: Advertising Your Properties

If you have hired a good professional screener, as I strongly recommended in the last chapter, chances are good that they have a solid marketing plan. Most have pretty good ads that they have tweaked for effectiveness over the years. Some use a cookie cutter approach so all they have to do is plug in your property information.

I like to stay out of the way and let my professionals do their jobs. They will usually advertise and market your property on all of the usual real estate websites. Everyone has access to just about all of the real estate sites these days.

In addition to the job my hired professionals are doing, I like to write a few ads of my own. As I mentioned before, these ads make the property look like a FSBO, so they attract people who might have otherwise overlooked the professional ad. I keep my ads short and to the point. I also include my screener's name and contact information in them.

Be Sure Your Screener is Prepared

Any time you are putting someone else's contact information in your ads, make sure that you run it by them first. I once posted an ad for a home that was just going on the market. In my haste, I forgot to tell my wonderful realtor/screener, Angela, that I was including her contact information in the ad.

Angela called me about a half an hour after the ad was posted. She told me that her phone was ringing off of the hook, and she just knew that it had to be because of me. I apologized. She was not upset — just caught off guard.

The professional screeners I use really like the fact that I enhance their marketing efforts.

Givers Get; Takers Do Not. Be a Giver.

Even after my homes are sold, I do not necessarily take the ads down. I tend let them run until they expire. Why, you might ask?

It's because prospects will continue to call. Even though the house they are calling about is off the market, my screener will usually have additional properties that are available. By leaving the ad up, I am giving my professional screener more leads and more contacts.

Experience has shown me that, in this business, you want to be known as a giver. Too many people who go into the real estate business do so as takers. You do not want the reputation as a taker.

I have found that the more you give, the more you get. Of course, you should always give without expectations of receiving anything in return. You will soon find that the people you are dealing with will start to respond in kind.

Also, if you are known as a giver, you will automatically move up on your screener's list of priorities. My screeners invariably return my calls and get my properties dealt with very quickly. It's not just my screeners and realtors who respond this way; it's everyone I deal with, from attorneys to insurance brokers. They all take care of me very well.

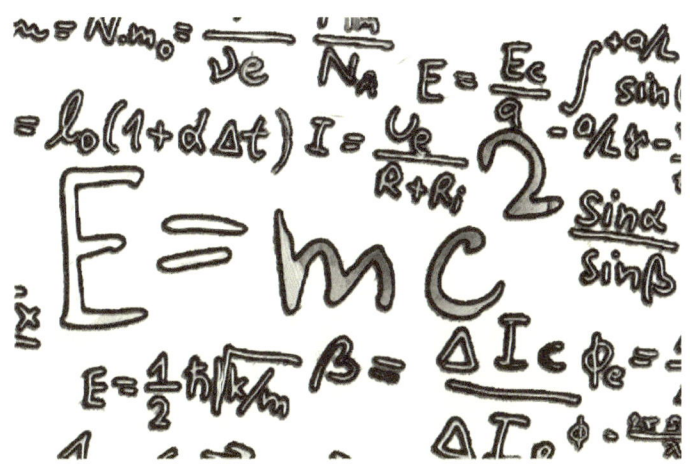

Keep Your Ads Simple and To-the-Point

So what kind of an ad do I usually post? I like to keep it brief and right to the point. I only put in enough information so that prospects will call for more details. Here's a sample:

Fire Your Landlord! Possible Owner Financing! Nice Home – Nice Area

Nice Home - Nice Area of Parkland MO - Now Available

2-bedroom 1 bath - Large fenced yard

Possible owner financing for the right person. Easy qualification.

Low down!

Only $997 per month! Cash price and special financing price at 0%interest

Call Angela now for details 314-555-3070

That's it. It's very simple and to-the-point. The prospective buyer needs to call for more detailed information. I also include a lot of pictures of the property. People love photos. The more pictures the better.

With more and more people searching for real estate on the Internet, you need to have lots of good-quality photos. The posted ads that don't have photos are usually skipped over.

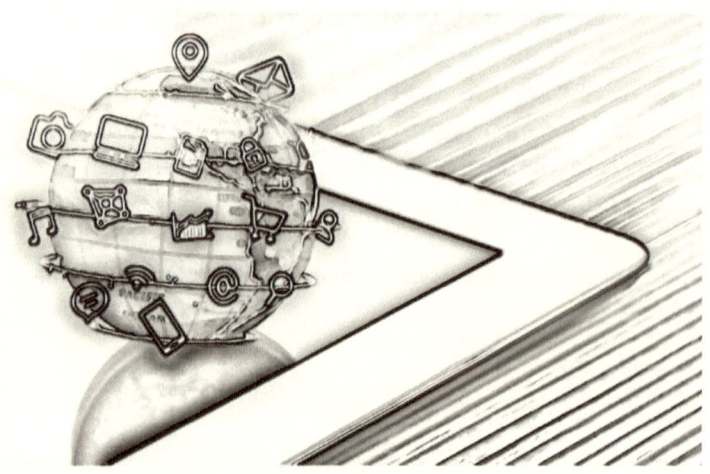

Control Your Marketing

You want to participate and control your marketing. You want to add value to your ads and benefit those who you have hired to be on your team. You want twenty-seven inquiries each day.

1 + 1 = 27

By running your own ads, you will increase the interest in your listings, and you will also add value to your professional screener's marketing arsenal. Keep it simple and be a giver. Trust me; you won't regret it.

"Words are our Most Inexhaustible Supply of Magic."
~ J.K. Rowling

In the next chapter, I will be showing you that you still get the final word about who buys your home.

Landlord Pennies...

To...

Banker Dollars...

Your Choice...

8. STEP 5: Who Gets the Final Word?

Chapter Eight

STEP 5: Who Gets the Final Word?

"Obviously, there's the temptation to sit back and smile... But there's so much at stake, we have to do our due diligence."

~Ralph Neas

By now, we have transformed our mindset from landlord to banker. We have owners and buyers instead of tenants. We know why the M.O.M. system is far better than the typical way most rent their houses. We have also gotten our properties in better than rent-ready and know our environment; and we have discovered why we want a professional to do our screening and how to enhance their marketing efforts.

We've covered a lot so far in just the first four simple and easy-to-follow steps. We only have a couple more steps to go over before you're on your way to an easier street. I say this lightly, as we all experience an abundance of easy and hard things in our lives. In this case, I'm just concerned with ensuring that your real estate investments to go as smoothly as possible.

And that's what the M.O.M. system is designed to do for you. Your life as a banker will be far more enjoyable than your previous life as a landlord. Once you have a buyer instead of a renter living in your investment home, you will eliminate most of the nightmares that go hand-in-hand with being a landlord.

So who gets the final word when it comes to selling your properties? This may seem like a dumb question. Of course, *you* get the final word. Sure, you can take your professional screener's recommendations, and there are often other factors that come into play, but ultimately, the final decision is yours and yours alone to make.

Here in Step Five, I will talk about getting the final word on who is chosen to become your new homeowner. Let's face it: the prospective buyers who are looking for owner-financed homes probably have a few dings on their credit reports.

Choosing the Right Buyers

So what are we looking for in those prospective buyers and homeowners? We are looking for someone who may have a bad credit report due to something that makes sense. If there happens to be a bankruptcy or foreclosure, we want to know the reason.

Did they go through a messy divorce that hurt them financially? Did they get hit with overwhelming medical bills at time when they were uninsured? Was there a death in the family that caused them to lose a significant portion of their household income? There are so many reasons why people's credit gets messed up. You just have to look between the lines and determine what situations make sense to you.

We all have different levels of risk tolerance when it comes to our investments. Some of us will take on more risk than others. In my experience, the biggest real estate investment risks I have taken have all involved my rental properties. I have eliminated most of my risks by adopting the M.O.M. system.

An Example of a Good Homebuyer

So, what do I look for when evaluating a potential homebuyer? As I said, I look for something that makes sense *to me*.

One of my screeners recently sent me an application wherein the applicant's credit score was very low. Looking into it, I found out that person had had some large medical bills in the past and he currently owed back child support payments.

By reading between the lines, I learned that the large medical bills this applicant had acquired prior to joining the military had greatly damaged his credit. Later, a complicated divorce had made a mess of his finances. Additionally, he had found it difficult to keep up with his child-support payments while he was waiting for his military pension to kick in.

At the time of his application, this applicant had begun collecting his pension, which totaled more than $3,500 a month. Also, he had worked out a deal through the courts and was making manageable payments on his back-child support.

He had recently moved to the area where my house was located in order to help care for his elderly grandmother, who needed some assistance around the house as well as rides to stores and doctor's appointments.

For the past eight months, this prospective buyer had been paying $900 a month to rent a very small apartment in a not-so-desirable neighborhood. This apartment was the only place he could find due to his financial circumstances. My screener told me that most of his other clients would not rent to him.

I thought that this guy's situation made sense. He had a good income and had worked out a payment plan on his back-child support. Also, he had been renting for a while with a solid payment record.

Additionally, making this purchase would be a good deal for this prospective buyer. His grandmother lived much closer to the house I was selling than to his apartment; and buying this house would actually save him money. Our monthly payment amount was only $797, which was $100 less than he was paying in rent.

Ok, so what about my side of the deal? How was this going to work out for me?

I had been renting this home out for several years at a rate of $650 per month. Over the years, I'd had some very good tenants as well as a few not-so-good ones. It goes with the territory. I was actually looking to sell this property outright since it was the last one I had left in this particular community.

Once I had gotten the property better than rent ready, I put a FSBO sign in the yard. Property values had gone down in this neighborhood since I had purchased the house. I got a couple of offers for $25,000 and $30,000 cash. I was not too thrilled about this considering I'd originally paid $55,000 for the property.

So, I decided to sell it through owner financing, and I hired a professional screener who found me this guy. We had listed the property at $55,900 cash, or at a special financing price of $99,900 with a low down-payment, 0% interest, and monthly payments of just $797. It was a Win/Win/Win situation for everyone involved.

After I accepted his application, my new homeowner paid a couple thousand dollars down plus two months' payments. He was able to buy a home that was close to his grandmother's, that cost him less than the rent he was paying on his small apartment, and that he would have had a hard time qualifying for had he made the purchase traditionally. Also, my professional screener received his fee immediately.

I got more money up front than I would have by renting out this home. I also got a higher monthly amount than I was collecting in rent, plus I do not have to deal with all the headaches that go along with property management, including such things as repairs, maintenance, taxes, and everything else that goes along with being a landlord. Furthermore, I can count on receiving a monthly income that will continue for about ten years.

Who Gets the Final Word?
You do.

The bottom line is you want to make deals that make sense to you. You also want everyone to win. If you follow the M.O.M. system, you will win more often than not. You will also make more money by being the banker than you can by being the landlord.

You still get the final word.

I don't say so because I'm so busy...I say so because I don't want to be so busy. ~John Lee

In the next chapter, I will show you how you can simplify the paperwork and keep it in your favor.

Landlord Pennies...

To...

Banker Dollars...

Your Choice...

9. STEP 6: K.I.S.R.S.

Chapter Nine

STEP 6: K.I.S.R.S.

"Mindfulness Living in the Moment Living in the Breath ~ Amit Ray

You're probably familiar with the acronym, K.I.S.S. "Keep It Simple, Silly." (Some people say, "Keep it simple, stupid," while others use even more colorful "s"-words. I prefer the use of the word "silly" myself.) The point is: it's never a good idea to over-complicate things. That notion actually seems kind of funny when it comes to real estate transactions.

So many people love to make real estate investing overly confusing. When I first became a mortgage broker (long before I moved into investing), I was amazed by the number of acronyms that are used in this industry. It almost seemed like everyone in the real estate world was trying to keep things shrouded in mystery.

At that time, I was determined to ensure that every one of my clients understood what they were doing in the very simplest of terms. Similarly, when I created the M.O.M. system, I decided to continue keeping things as simple as possible.

In accordance with the philosophy that it's best to use what has always seemed to work well, I advise you to K.I.S.R.S., or "Keep It Simple — Really Simple." I cannot express enough the importance of keeping everything simple with the M.O.M. system — especially when it comes to paperwork. It is crucial that everyone involved in the deal understands what's going on.

Again, let me stress that *I am not an attorney* and I am not an expert on the law. I am therefore not capable of giving you any kind of legal or professional advice. For that, you should consult an attorney of your own. I am just going to show you what I do and what has worked well for me. Talk to your lawyer before doing the same, as laws can differ according to location and situation.

Over the years, through much trial and much error, I have simplified my real estate paperwork as it pertains to the M.O.M. system. With the help of my attorney, I have attempted to cover all of the bases, and have made the changes and simplified the processes when appropriate.

Most property managers, screeners, and realtors already have their own standard paperwork that they use. I always let the professionals that I hire use their own application form and screening process. They send me a selection of prospective homebuyers, and I stay out of their way until I get an applicant that makes sense. Then, I take over using my own paperwork.

I keep my paperwork as simple as possible so that it is easy for everyone to understand. I do not want there to be any misunderstandings, and I want everything to be known upfront.

When doing a M.O.M. system deal, it is important to make it clear that you will not be giving back any deposits or any other monies received like you did when you were a landlord. You are now the banker, and bankers are not in the habit of giving back money.

You'll want to only use a handful of documents and agreements, and you'll want to keep it simple. You do not want your buyer to have dozens of papers to sign like with a traditional bank loan.

Don't confuse your homebuyer. A confused mind always say no.

At the time of closing, the forms I use include:

- a one-page sales contract,
- a one-page CFD (contract for deed),
- a lease,
- a lead-based paint poisoning notification,
- an authorization to release information,
- and, in many cases, two QCD's (quit claim deeds). I'll explain this further later on.

On the following pages, I will provide for information about these forms as well as samples of each so that you can get an idea of what they look like and how much information is included in each.

Again, I recommend consulting an attorney before putting your paperwork together.

The Sales Agreement

I use a very simple one-page sales agreement. It spells out the terms of the deal in easy-to-understand language. It is not confusing.

CONTRACT TO PURCHASE REAL ESTATE

BE IT KNOWN, the undersigned Grace Watson (Buyer), agrees to purchase from Heartland Property Sellers, Inc._ (Owner), real estate known as 201 Anderson Street, City/Town of ST Louis, County of St Louis, State of Missouri, said property more particularly described as:

Loc. Number : 10G0231801
Bradley Sub.: lot 1 & 2 Blk 28 Pb 26 Pg 18
202 Anderson Street
St Louis MO 63127

The purchase priced agreed is $___199,900__ Financed by owner

Deposit herewith paid	$__3,000_____
Balance of terms - Transaction Cost	$_196,900_____
Total:	$_199,900_____
	Total

This contract is conditional upon the following terms:

1. This contract is for purchase of said property in "as is" condition.

2. Other terms:

2019 Taxes will be prorated

Signed this _____ day of _____, 2019.

Buyer_____ Date_____

Buyer_____ Date_____

Seller__*John Lee of* HPS INC _____ Date_____, 2019____

Seller_____ Date_____

The CFD (Contract for Deed)

This is a sample of my CFD, or contract for deed. Again, it's a one-page agreement that's easy to understand. In some states, you will need to use a land contract instead. It is essentially the same thing with slightly different wording. You'll need to find out what is appropriate for your area.

This CFD spells out the terms of the sale clearly. It also specifies that the purchaser is responsible for the taxes and insurance.

Contract For Deed

This agreement constitutes a purchase of the property below by the undersigned:

Bradley Sub Lot 1 & 2 Blk 28
202 Anderson St
St Louis MO 63127

The following provisions and stipulations are a part of this agreement:

Sales price is $_199,900_. Purchaser will pay a nonrefundable down payment of $ 3,000.00 _ and Monthly payments of **$997**, at **0%**.
Payments are due on the _ **20**th _ of each month beginning April _ 20 _, 2019

Payments Not received by the due date are subject to a **5%** late charge. Upon satisfactory repayment the seller will execute and deliver unto the purchaser a special warranty deed conveying title in fee simple to the subject property.

In the event all agreed payments are not paid in a timely manner, i.e. three months in arrears, then the purchasers forfeit all claims to the subject property. The seller may re-enter and take full possession of the subject property. Checks returned from your bank for any reason will result in an additional **$49** charge. This property may be paid in full at any time with no prepayment penalty.

In the event purchaser can obtain other financing, upon receipt of the payoff funds, the seller will execute and deliver unto the purchaser a special warranty deed conveying title in fee simple to the subject property.

Taxes and Insurance are to be paid by the purchaser.

Purchaser   GRACE WATSON   Date

Purchaser _____   Date

John Lee
Seller Heartland Property Sellers INC   Date
Member of the Management Team John Lee

The Lease

I use a simple, standard lease, similar to the one I would use if I were renting out the house instead of selling it. The one I use is not unique. You can find these on the Internet or any business supply store.

The lease is necessary if, for some reason, you need to take the property back non-voluntarily. The CFD *does* spell out that after three months of no payments, the buyer agrees to give back the property voluntarily; but it is better to have a legal document to back you up if you must force an eviction.

Fortunately, I have never had to do this.

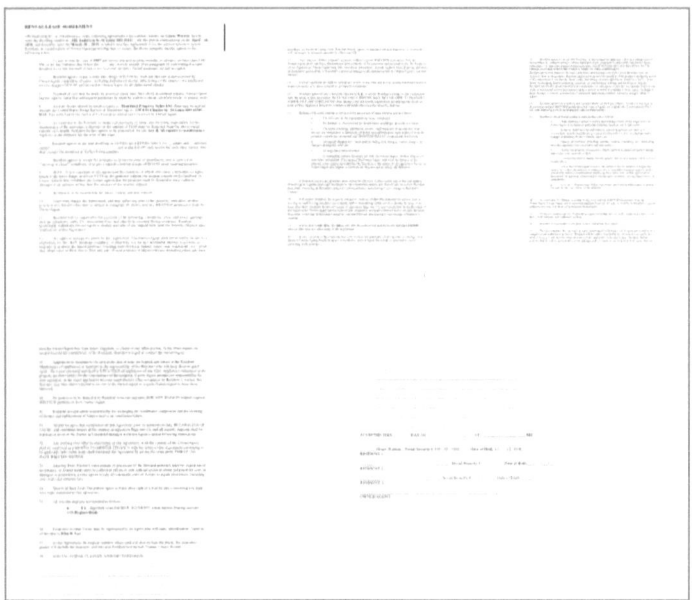

The Lead-Based Paint Poisoning Notification

Don't forget the lead-based paint poisoning notification. If the house you are selling was built prior to 1978, you are required by federal law to supply the buyer with this information.

Lead-Based Paint Disclosure

Federal law requires that every landlord must sign this form with their tenant prior to leasing their home if it was constructed before 1978, and provide the tenant with information about lead and its hazards. To obtain a brochure published by the Environmental Protection Agency, entitled *Protect Your family from Lead in Your Home* that meets the requirements of the law, contact:

National Lead Information Center and Clearinghouse
8601 Georgia Avenue, Suite 503
Silver Springs, MD 20910
(800) 424-LEAD
http://www.epa.gov/lead/nlic.htm

Have your attorney review this and all forms before you use them.

(Rentals and Leases) Disclosure of Information on Lead-Based Paint and Lead-Based Paint Hazards

Lead Warning Statement

Housing built before 1978 may contain lead-based paint. Lead from paint, paint chips and dust can pose health hazards if not taken care of properly. Lead exposure is especially harmful to young children and pregnant women. Before renting pre-1978 housing, landlords must disclose the presence of known lead-based paint and lead-based paint hazards in the dwelling. Tenants must also receive a federally approved pamphlet on lead poisoning prevention.

Lessor's Disclosure (initial)

(a) Presence of lead-based paint and/or lead-based paint hazards (check one)

_____ Known lead-based paint and/or lead-based paint hazards are present in the housing (explain).

_____

_____ Lessor has no knowledge of lead-based paint and/or lead-based paint hazards in the housing.

(b) Records and reports available to the lessor (check one)

_____ Lessor has provided the lessee with all available records and reports pertaining to lead-based paint and/or lead-based paint hazards in the housing (list the documents).

_____

_____ Lessor has no reports or records pertaining to lead-based paint and/or lead-based paint hazards in the housing.

Lessee's Acknowledgment (initial)

(c) Lessee has received copies of all information listed above.

(d) Lessee has received the pamphlet *Protect Your Family from Lead in Your Home*.

Certification of Accuracy

The following parties have reviewed the information above and certify, to the best of their knowledge, that the information provided by the signatory is true and accurate.

Lessor	Date	Lessee	Date
Lessor	Date	Lessee	Date

The Authorization to Release Information

You will absolutely want to have an authorization to release information agreement on file. Should you ever have a need to verify any information provided by your buyer, this form is a must.

No one will talk to you about your purchaser's personal information without this signed form. Nor should they.

Authorization To Release Information

Lender:_____

Lender Contact Phone #:_____

Loan/Account Number:_____

Property Address:_____

I/We hereby authorize you to release to _____ or its agents and assigns any and all information that they may require for the transfer or payoff concerning my loan/account for the above referenced property. "Agents" shall include all real estate agents, attorneys, and their assistants.

_____   _____   _____
Borrower's Signature   **Social Security #**   **Date**

Printed Name:_____

_____   _____   _____
Co-Borrower's Signature   **Social Security #**   **Date**

Printed Name:_____

The QCD (Quit Claim Deed)

Often (though not always), I provide **two** Quit Claim Deeds. One QCD is from the seller (the *Grantor*) to the buyer (the *Grantee*); and the other QCD is from the buyer (Grantee) back to us as the seller (Grantor). This form does require us to go before a notary, so it is a bit more troublesome than the others.

There are a couple of reasons this form can prove important. Some municipalities will not recognize your new homeowner as the owner of the property based strictly on your paperwork. They will require a deed be recorded in the buyer's name.

If your new buyer wants to have work done on the house and needs to get a permit, or if they have an ordinance violation filed against them, the city may still consider you to be the property owner. This form puts ownership of the property in your buyer's name. Furthermore, it allows the county to send the tax bill directly to the buyers when property taxes are due.

So why would you get a second QCD going in the other direction? In short, it's for your protection. Instead of submitting this form to be recorded right away, you should put it away in your file. In the event that something goes wrong and you need to get the property back, having this form already prepared can save you a lot of frustration since it is almost impossible to get your buyer to sign paperwork after a deal goes south.

Let's say that after five years of making payments, your homeowners get divorced and the ex-husband moves out of the area. The wife may not be able to afford to keep the home because of her financial situation. In this case, it would be extremely difficult to get both parties to sign a QCD to transfer ownership of the property back to you. If you already have a QCD on file, this is one less headache you have to deal with.

My attorney advised that I get both of these QCD's notarized upfront. This is very good advice. I have never had to go this route, and do not plan on ever needing to. It's still better to be prepared and safe than sorry.

Here is a sample of the Grantor to Grantee QCD I use:

QUITCLAIM DEED

THIS QUITCLAIM DEED, Executed this ____ day of _____, 2019,

by the Grantor,   Heartland Property Sellers INC, whose mailing address is
       135 S. St. Charles St., St. Louis MO 63307-8119

to the Grantee,   Grace Watson, whose mailing address is
       770 Maryville Ave, St Louis MO 63167

WITNESSETH,

That the said Grantor, for and in consideration of the sum of Ten Dollars and other valuable consideration paid by the said Grantee, the receipt whereof is hereby acknowledged, does hereby remise, release and quitclaim unto the said Grantee forever, all the right, title, interest and claim which the said Grantor has in and to the following described parcel of land, and improvements and appurtenances thereto in the County of St. Francois, State of Missouri, to wit:

Legal Disc: **Locator number 10G0231801, Bradley Sub Lot 1 & 2 Pb 26 Pg 18, St Louis County, Missouri– COMMONLY KNOWN AS: 202 Anderson St, St Louis MO 63127**

Subject to all building lines, conditions, restrictions and easements of record, if any.

IN WITNESS WHEREOF, The said Grantee has signed and sealed these presents the day and year first above written.

Signed, sealed and delivered in presence of:

Grantor John Lee of Heartland Property Sellers INC   Grantee Grace Watson

STATE OF
}

COUNTY OF
}

On this _____ day of _____, 2019, before me personally appeared

_____, personally known to me (or proved to me on the basis of satisfactory evidence) to be the person(s) whose name(s) is/are subscribed to the within instrument and acknowledged to me that he/she/they executed the same in his/her/their authorized capacity(ies), and that by his/her/their signature(s) on the instrument the person(s), or the entity upon behalf of which the person(s) acted, executed the instrument.

WITNESS my hand and official seal

Notary Public

My term expires:

And here is the QCD from our buyers back to us:

QUITCLAIM DEED

THIS QUITCLAIM DEED, Executed this ____ day of _____, 2019,

by the Grantor,   Grace Watson, whose mailing address is
770 Maryville Ave, St Louis MO 63167

to the Grantee,   Heartland Property Sellers INC, whose mailing address is
135 S St Charles St., St. Louis MO 63307-8119

WITNESSETH,

That the said Grantor, for and in consideration of the sum of Ten Dollars and other valuable consideration paid by the said Grantee, the receipt whereof is hereby acknowledged, does hereby remise, release and quitclaim unto the said Grantee forever, all the right, title, interest and claim which the said Grantor has in and to the following described parcel of land, and improvements and appurtenances thereto in the County of St. Francois, State of Missouri, to wit:

Legal Disc. **Locator number 10G0231801, Bradley Sub Lot 1 & 2 Pb 21 Pg 8, St Louis County, Missouri– COMMONLY KNOWN AS: 202 Anderson St, St Louis MO 63127**

Subject to all building lines, conditions, restrictions and easements of record, if any

---

IN WITNESS WHEREOF, The said Grantee has signed and sealed these presents the day and year first above written

Signed, sealed and delivered in presence of

_____   _____
Grantor Grace Watson   Grantee John Lee of Heartland Sellers INC

STATE OF
]
COUNTY OF
]

On this ____ day of _____, 2019, before me personally appeared

_____, personally known to me (or proved to me on the basis of satisfactory evidence) to be the person(s) whose name(s) is/are subscribed to the within instrument and acknowledged to me that he/she/they executed the same in his/her/their authorized capacity(ies), and that by his/her/their signature(s) on the instrument the person(s), or the entity upon behalf of which the person(s) acted, executed the instrument.

WITNESS my hand and official seal

_____
Notary Public

My term expires

In Conclusion:

So in a nutshell, that's all of the paperwork that you need to close a deal. Through many years of trials and errors, I have simplified the M.O.M. system's paperwork and processes many times over. I am very happy with my system as it now stands.

I highly recommend that you make sure that whatever you are doing is in full compliance with the laws in your municipality, city, and state. If need be, seek the advice of a local professional.

Remember, K.I.S.R.S.

Keep It Simple — Really Simple. You won't regret it.

"Life is Joyfully Simple. Keep it That Way."
~ Paul Jun

In the next chapter, I will be going over my favorite part of the M.O.M. system: collecting the money as a banker, not as a landlord. Oh yeah, and also relaxing!

Landlord Pennies...

To...

Banker Dollars...

Your Choice...

10. STEP 7: Landlords Work Hard... Bankers Collect Easily

Chapter Ten

STEP 7: Landlords Work Hard...
Bankers Collect Easily

"Success at Anything Will Always Come Down to This: Focus & Effort, and We Control Both."
~ Dewayne Johnson (The Rock)

Do you want to work hard like a landlord, or would you rather collect easily like a banker?

Hmm. Let me think about that... I think I'll take the nine-to-five, not working too hard, money-collecting life of a banker, thank you very much. What about you? It's your choice.

Know Your Why's

Now we're at the final step of the M.O.M. system: collecting your money. This is really why we are in this business, isn't it? All of us have different reasons for wanting and needing money. We all have different 'why's.' Why do *you* want and need money?

For some of us, our *why* is the lifestyle we want to live. For me, it's about freedom. I don't have to depend on anyone else financially. I have the freedom to live the lifestyle I choose. I get to do what I want, when I want, and with whom I want.

What is your *why*? Maybe you want freedom like I do. Maybe you want more for your family and loved ones. Maybe you just want to be able to pay the bills on time. Whatever your reason for being in this business, it's important that you know your *why*.

There was a time in my life when I thought it was all about the money. Then I experienced one of those major life changes that seem to come around every five to seven years.

In 2007, my beautiful wife, Sue, was diagnosed with stage-four colon cancer. The diagnosis came on March 1st, and she passed away on June 27th. We could not have predicted that, and certainly did not see it coming.

What I discovered the hard way is the true value of financial freedom.

Unlike most people in my situation, I did not have to go to a job every day. I was able to be with my wife through all of her medical treatments and procedures. The ability to spend all of that precious time with her during her final moments was a priceless gift. Most people do not have that luxury. And yes, it is a luxury.

When you know what you value most in life, you come to understand your *why's*.

The Easily-Collecting Banker

Being the easily-collecting banker instead of the hard-working landlord gives you much more freedom to live your life the way you want to live it. You don't have to think twice about what is important to you or where your time is best spent.

Collecting money like a banker is easy and fun. Every day is a holiday. Oh sure, there are still some things in life you're going to have to deal with that are not easy. But handling your various daily problems is much easier when you don't have to worry about money coming in or little things like paying the bills.

Collecting the proceeds from your investments is a very easy thing to do. I collect money a few different ways. I'm pretty much open to any way someone wants to give it to me. I'll accept checks, money orders, Square, eChecks, PayPal, Venmo, or any other form of payment.

Many people prefer to pay electronically these days. Some services such as Square and PayPal charge you a service fee. This can range anywhere from 2.9% to about 3.2%. That's okay. It's the cost of doing business. Do keep in mind, these fees are tax-deductible.

I still have a lot of buyers who send me checks and money orders each month. Yes, I still get money orders. Something I started doing many years ago for these buyers is to include a pre-addressed, stamped envelope with the confirmation (receipt) I mail them each month. It makes life a little easier for them.

I give my buyers a confirmation of their investment instead of a receipt for their payment. Little differences in the words we use can improve the way people see things. Would you rather invest in your home or make a payment? Would you rather have a confirmation of your investment or a receipt for your monthly installment? It's not always what you say, it's how you say it.

Using a 0% interest rate keeps our math very simple. The problem I have always had with amortization tables is that they are not always easy for people to understand. Many buyers are confused by the change in the amount of interest charged from month to month.

Simple math is easy to understand. If you owe me $100,000 and pay me $1,000, you owe me $99,000. If you're paying me 6.5% interest on the $100,000 debt, how much do you owe me each month? Keep it K.I.S.R.S. You'll be glad you did.

One of the things that I've developed with the M.O.M. system over the years is giving my buyers the option of paying off their remaining debt in full with financial incentives. I offer a 10% discount off the total balance, **or** they can pay the original cash price, whichever is less.

Keep in mind that the original *cash price* is usually only a bit higher than market value, while our *financing price* is typically **much** higher than actual market value. Therefore, there is room for big savings for my buyers if they suddenly come into money or are able to acquire a loan that will enable them to pay off the debt at a significantly reduced price.

To date, none of my buyers has paid me off earlier than the terms of their note. Even when they get the balance down and have the potential to save ten percent, they don't take the offer.

Most of my buyers pay early each month. The postpaid envelope that I send with their confirmation makes it easy. Lots of my buyers have told me how much they appreciate my providing this little extra service.

When was the last time one of your creditors sent you a postpaid envelope with one of your bills? I don't think I have ever gotten one.

I usually hand write something on the confirmation too like, "Thank You!!!" And I like to add a gold star next to the buyer's name. Gold stars are an inexpensive way to add a nice touch.
Anything you do that no one else does makes you stand out.

Who wouldn't want to invest with someone who values them with a gold star? You want to stand out, and you want to get paid.

Here is a copy of the confirmation I send, as well as the postpaid envelope I include with it:

November 2, 2019

Received from ▇▇▇▇▇▇▇▇▇▇▇▇▇▇▇▇

Investment of: check/mo/cash/paypal/echeck of **$1150** *

Property address: 9▇▇▇▇▇▇▇ St Charles MO 63067-1106

Any balance due **$ 180,055.75** *

Next regular investment of **$1150** is due on **01 / 01 /2020**

Please Allow Time for Mailing

Thank you,

John Lee
Management Team

Heartland Property Sellers INC
135 S. St Charles St
St Louis MO 63307-8119
314-555-1717
ams826@yahoo.com

"Due to your VIP status we will still honor your 10% discount when you choose to make the full investment today" Thank you"

HPSINC
135 S St Charles St
St Louis MO 63307-8119

Heartland Property Sellers INC
135 S St Charles St
St Louis MO 63307-8119

As you can see, the confirmation and the postpaid envelope are very simple and easy to understand. There's absolutely no reason for our buyers to not send in the payment on their investments each month.

Automatic transfers to your bank, PayPal, and Square are good ways to get your money, also. Square is a service that allows you to collect your money from your buyers' debit or credit cards. Like PayPal, Square charges a service fee. You will still get your money.

When it is all said and done, at the end of the day you can have an easy 9 to 5 job, or you can be on call 24 hours a day.

Landlords Work Hard...

Bankers Collect Easily...Period.

"Life is Really Simple, but We Insist on Making it Complicated."
~ Confucius

Next and last, but at the same time not least:

Landlord Pennies…

To…

Banker Dollars...

Your Choice...

11. $ 🖤 ☺ ☮ 🎵 🌴 2 U !

Chapter Eleven

$ ♥ ☺ ☮ ♫ 🌴 2 U !

"Paradise is Open to All Kind Hearts."
~ Pierre-Jean de Beranger

Okay, so now that you are a banker and not a landlord, I want to leave you with a special prediction. Your life will be less stressful, and you will collect your money easier. You'll have more time to spend doing what you want, with whom you want, when you want — just like I do.

You will not be taking maintenance calls from renters. You will not be collecting late fees from tenants. You will not be dealing with leaking pipes and code violations. You will not be dealing with what I call the Dreaded 3-T's of Landlording: toilets, trash and tenants.

The title of this chapter is what I want for you. I put these symbols on my business cards. Well, I *used to*, I should say. I actually I haven't used business cards in many years. People rarely keep business cards, so why bother with something that is normally thrown away?

I hand out million-dollar bills with my contact information on them. I have given away about two billion dollars since I started doing this. My million-dollar bills have these symbols on them; and they are my special message to you. I want the best for you.

You deserve much $ = money in your life.

You deserve much ♥ = love in your life.

You deserve much ☺ = happiness in your life.

You deserve much ☮ = peace in your life.

You deserve much ♪ = harmony in your life.

You deserve much 🌴 = paradise in your life.

Because of the Deal'ionaire M.O.M. System
You Are No
Longer a Landlord.

Because of the Deal'ionaire M.O.M. System
You Are
Now a Banker!

Because of the Deal'ionaire M.O.M System
We All Win/Win/Win!!

Because of the Deal'ionaire M.O.M. System

You Deserve So Much More:

$  2 U !

You may think the grass is greener on the other side, but if you take the time to water your own grass, it will be just as green.

"You Must Unlearn What You Have Learned…~Yoda"

More books written by: John Lee

Secrets of a Deal'ionaire

Creating Wealth One Small Deal at a Time

Foreword By *Robert Allen* – Multiple NY Times Best-selling author

"The reader cannot escape the conclusion the author knows his subject matter. I thought the government was the only one to make money out of taxes!" –William B. Beedie, Attorney

"In his new book, *Secrets of a Deal'ionaire*, John Lee teaches unique strategies for buying real estate with little or no money. *Secrets of a Deal'ionaire* is the 21st century's new book of *Nothing Down*." AJ Rassamni, author of Gain the Unfair Advantage

© HHLLC 2014, 2019. Secrets of a Deal'ionaire. Deal'ionaire OTC System Premier Signature Series. All Rights Reserved.

Another Book by:

John Lee

Secrets Those Credit Doctors Don't Want You to Know

7 Simple Steps to a Higher Credit Score

© HHLLC 2014, 2019. Secrets of a Deal'ionaire. Deal'ionaire OTC System Premier Signature Series. All Rights Reserved.

Accompanying Workbook for the Credit Book by:

John Lee

Secrets Those Credit Doctors Don't Want You to Know Workbook

This is a must have accompanying workbook for *Secrets Those Credit Doctors Don't Want You to Know* that takes you step by step to a higher credit score.

© HHLLC 2014, 2019. Secrets of a Deal'ionaire. Deal'ionaire OTC System
Premier Signature Series. All Rights Reserved.

About the Author John Lee the Deal'ionaire

John R Lee has been investing in unconventional, unique real estate deals for over 25 years. He was a mortgage broker for many years and also has an extensive insurance background. He's been around the block more than once. John's also written several best-selling books including, "Secrets of a Deal'ionaire" and "Secrets THOSE Credit Doctors Don't Want YOU to Know."

Today, Lee focuses on education and stresses how important it is for you to succeed. One of the most important things John has learned is to get a mentor and jump-start your way to success. As he always says, "There are two ways to do things, the easy way or the hard way. A mentor will get you there the easy way. The hard way is to spend twenty-five years learning it by yourself. Investing is a team-sport."

John is most famous for showing you how to turn $200 into $2,000 with about 2 hours' worth of work. By doing so you can spend more time with your loved ones and doing things you want to do, like he does.

The secrets and strategies John share are unique and priceless. He has simplified processes that can be very complicated.

© HHLLC 2014, 2019. Secrets of a Deal'ionaire. Deal'ionaire OTC System Premier Signature Series. All Rights Reserved

What Others are Saying...

I've been a landlord for over 30 years and know all of the stress that goes with it. I know use the M.O.M. system and have time to travel and see my grandkids, which is really what I always wanted to do. ~ Christopher L. – St. Joseph MO

I'm fairly new to real estate investing. With only three rental properties I didn't have any free time. Now that I discovered the M.O.M. system I have time to go to my kids' ballgames, spend time with my new baby and enjoy my life. ~ Brooke W. – Chicago IL

Being a property manager for over 20 years, I have seen the good, the bad and the ugly of land lording. After sharing John's program with some long-time landlords, they cannot thank me enough. My only concern is these techniques may put me out of a job. Good thing John and I have been friends for many years. ~ Cindi P. – St. Louis MO

To find out more about:

John Lee **and the Deal'ionaire's latest books and upcoming events, visit**

www.theDEALIONAIRE.com

You may also email John directly at

theDEALIONAIRE@gmail.com

© HHLLC 2014, 2019. Secrets of a Deal'ionaire. Deal'ionaire OTC System Premier Signature Series. All Rights Reserved.

www.ingramcontent.com/pod-product-compliance
Lightning Source LLC
Chambersburg PA
CBHW021405210526
45463CB00001B/234